WHERE ALL THINGS MEET, MIRROR & MINGLE

WHERE ALL THINGS MEET, MIRROR & MINGLE

POEMS BY

Catherine Lawton

CLADACH
Publishing

© 2025 Catherine Lawton

An AGATES Book of Poetry

CLADACH Publishing
Greeley, Colorado
https://cladach.com

Cover Photo:
  John Timothy Watkin
Interior Art:
  Beau Slike
Interior Photos:
  pp. 2, 6: John Timothy Watkin; pp. 10, 24, 42, 98: Catherine Lawton;
  p. 58: Michael Hallanan/Unsplash; p. 72: Larry Lawton;
  p. 112: Beverly Coons

All rights reserved.

Paperback ISBN: 9781945099403

When asked 'What color is your poetry?'... I answer:

    Silver—
        for the lining of the clouds
        the shining of the lake
        the rising of the mist
        the sprighting of the stars

CONTENTS

I. *SEEN & UNSEEN* 11
    At the Pond 13
    Dispelled 14
    Bearings 15
    The Light That Is 16
    You In Me and I In You 17
    Burning Bush Tree 18
    Without Memory We Have No Future 20
    We Cannot Stay There 22
    Recognition and Response 23

II. *CYCLES & SEASONS* 25
    Wonders Observed 27
    The Long Cold Stare of January 28
    Holy Stillness 29
    Enchanted February 30
    As Days Lengthen 31
    Humming Together 32
    Hymn of Spring After a Long Winter 33
    The Ins and Outs of March 34
    Backyard Observations In Late March 35
    Fellowship at the Feeder 36
    May 2020 37
    Such a Tree 38
    Haiku 39
    Mottles and Dapples of a Fading Season 40
    Down by the Seashore 41

III. *BEEN & BECOMING* 43
    A Morning Prayer 45

Together Becoming 46
A Process 47
Witness 48
Campmeeting in the Hills 49
Glory 50
The Soul Likes Slow 51
No Forced Entry 52
Searching 53
Wounds 54
Be(e) Doing Good 55
Waking the Dead 56
Jesus In You? 57

IV. *TIME & SPACE* 59
    W.A.I. 61
    Wings 62
    Courage In 63
    Bridge 64
    Making 65
    That Close 66
    Shared Space In Time 67
    It's the Soul That's Solid 68
    God Was There and ... 69
    Fragmented 70
    Death Came Close That November 71

V. *INSIDE & OUT* 73
    Words 75
    Gates 76
    Till We Show Our Faces 78
    Unhealthy Atmosphere 80
    Questions Worth Asking 81
    Playing God 82
    Conflicted? 83
    Perfecting Perfectionism 84
    Spiraling 85

Doubting the Darkness 86
2020s Vision 88
Treasures of Darkness 89
Sincerity 90
Poetic Freedom or Unblocked 91
The Deeps Awake 92
Which Pre-Position? 93
Unquenchable Shining 94
Churned 95
In the Grasses 96

Notes 99
Acknowledgments 111
About 112

SEEN & UNSEEN

AT THE POND

Branches reaching upward
    search for roots.
Clouds floating on air
    bloat on water.
Sunrays light on ripples
    of perspective.
Rock tips speak of hidden
    range of memory.
Dragonflies wing in spray
    of jumping fish.
Above, below, they feed
    on tiny flies.
All things meet and mirror,
    seen and unseen.

DISPELLED

I dream that something looms—
 At my feet I see its shadow,
 feel it cold upon my back.

I wake, and then I ask—
 Can evil cast a shadow
 sans Sun behind the gloom?

BEARINGS

A Voice—through the fog caressing land,
    shrouding this place where I stand—
it calls, like the plaints of mourning dove coos
    and eery, sweet song of loons.

Beclouded here, timeless, I could be
    anywhere—on a desert, in trees,
on windblown strand of coastal cliff—
    hearing a Whisper in the mist.

What to believe—my ears, my eyes—
    under these tear-blurred skies?
But again, the ancient, relentless song
    reminds me of where I belong.

The longing here, the lure out there
call deep to deep, wed earth and air.

THE LIGHT THAT IS

Within this dim-world plight
One pure and living Flame
Exudes undying Light
Illumines every name.

We've not struck a match
Or lit a blaze for all
Or unlocked a flameproof hatch
Or 'let the fire fall.'

The Light of the world: It Is.
It spoke and now It speaks.
It penetrates. It wins.
It shows, reveals, and seeks.

Too bright for your dim eyes?
Prefer your masked disguise?
How long?

YOU IN ME AND I IN YOU

Why this sense of separateness,
  pulled by roughing riptides,
  trying to find channels,
  stay afloat, not capsize—?

When truly there's a stream
  running through my depths,
  now underground, now in sun,
  flowing on pebbled beds;

Now zigging, now zagging,
  ever drawn from divide
  toward sunrise, sunset,
  to plenteous welcoming tide.

As sapling roots seek communion
  in intertwined, forested place;
  as a smile resolves into laughter,
  as a touch melts in embrace;

As a honeybee homes in on colony
  after foraging far, alone,
  caught in storms but now re-orienting,
  always hoping against hope—

I flow to You, reach for You, fly into You.
  .

BURNING BUSH TREE

The Cross—which
before had stood splintery, brittle,
wooden, weathered—now glowed
blood-red, red-hot, molten.

We who wore small, cold crosses
hanging from our necks
felt them burn into our chests.
We who gazed at the tree
with eyes of hungry hearts
fell face to the ground,
then looked up, for a shadow fell round—
no, emanated—but not gray or darkening—
warm and intense, as if composed of light,
though not projected or reflected.
A Light that IS was manifest there.

Just above the enravished cross, cosmic
primal flares reached, streamed and—
like silent sunrays through ancient forest—
emblazoned, gilded the weighted tree.

Rising, heart thrilling, I stood,
arms extended like horizontal branches basking,
then grasping hands beside mine.
Our voices joined—with earth and air,
below, above—the all-encompassing,
soul-caressing song of Love.

Could I myself be desired and wooed so?
Surely truth resides in this Light though.
Barefoot, we root here and flourish together—
a forest of praise, sending seedlings, joining
the luminous chorus of forever becoming.

WITHOUT MEMORY WE HAVE NO FUTURE

We look, you and I, to our past
not to wrestle it interminably
but to find pattern for the present
and shape for the future.

The past, though settled, isn't dead.
Always it lies under the surface,
now and then erupting in memory or
startling with befuddling behaviors.

Beneath fallen leaves blanketing snow,
the past holds seeds deep that—
when conditions are favorable—
send up shoots to light of day.

Will we scythe or plow them under?
Or neglect rampant undergrowth
till wildfires blaze and raze and
phase out hopes of a future?

Hope will rise again though.
The Blood and Water that flowed
into all things humus now hums
a growing, re-generative love song.

What passed is past. The present is a present.
Potential futures arise, again and again,
out of composting history, re-seeding,
beckoning ... always wholeness making..

WE CANNOT STAY THERE

Don't spurn the past
but learn what lasts.
Like a thousand years is yesterday,
and I cry a thousand tears today.

Like the grass we fade away.
Like a dream we cannot stay
in palls of settledness:
We're called to wakefulness.

RECOGNITION AND RESPONSE

Deep calls to deep
  at the sound of Your waves.
Deep calls to deep
  in the warmth of Your light.
Deep calls to deep
  in the stir of Your breath.
Depth calls to depth
  like the sea to deep springs.
In the depths of my humanity
  Your voice reaches me.
I follow Your rays
  till Your Breath in me sings.

CYCLES & SEASONS

WONDERS OBSERVED

In Connecticut woods I've seen
fireflies flit, flash, and blink.

On O'ahu I've seen mighty waves
swell into tunneled highways.

On Redwood coast I've searched for
gems and jetsom washed ashore.

In Portland I've seen rain freeze
midair into sparkles crystaline.

THE LONG COLD STARE OF JANUARY

A *captive* to granite gray stare
I shiver and hunker there.

Clouds shudder also and
shake loose frozen crystals
flashing slivered light.

Now silver gleam the gazing eyes.
I rise, unblinking, *captivated.*

HOLY STILLNESS

There is no heartbeat
in a seed—
Yet life waits
in that brittle encasement
as surely as in the stilled
breathing and slowed
beating heart
of toads and salamanders
in winter deeps and
sleeping bears in caves.

Waiting, waiting, we wait
in lengthened nights and
chilled soil and cloistered suns
for warmer, lighter, moister days
to dawn.
From on high—and pulsing
in the depths—we hear
"Wait... Wait... Be still..."
and "Coming—
I have, I am, I will."

ENCHANTED FEBRUARY

Even though you know
more rain, snow
cold nights may come,
relish
red hearts, sweet confections,
melodies of friendship and love,
'faux spring' days so rare
of humming earth and hinting air;
watch
for swelling buds, first blooms;
with Faith (eyes open to mercies)
and Hope (eternally springing)
and the greatest, the essence,
Love, which sang the world into being.

May we—this late winter—
awaken
to things forgotten since the days
when the Singing, still listened for,
was known in the body of snow
as well as in the blood of rose.
The chant of red Love—may we
hear
and answer within all seasons.

AS DAYS LENGTHEN

The night will shake
 off chill,
The birds will take
 more color.
The grass will wake
 and green.
When Winter breaks
 into Spring.
The ice will crack
 on the pond.
And we will make
 an arbor
For Silver Lace
 to twine on.

HUMMING TOGETHER

You the humus,
I the human;
Together we're humming
A tune of becoming.

Responding to seasons,
Laughing at teasings
Of freezes, of dryness;
Working deepest for highest.

HYMN OF SPRING AFTER A LONG WINTER

Warm winds stir and rushes whisper:
   'We survived! We survived!'
Birds grow fatter, brighter, twitter:
   'We're alive! We're alive!'
Weeping willows leaf with laughter:
   'Water to drink! Water to drink!'

Bulbs have poked up bright surprises:
   'See our yellows, reds, and pink!'
Grass in lawn and field arises:
   'We're reviving! We're reviving!'
Trees now swell with buds of promise:
   'We are thriving! We are thriving!'

Rivers flow with rhyme and meter:
   'We have thawed from mount to plain!'
All respond to their Creator
   Who calls forth the Spring again.

THE INS AND OUTS OF MARCH

March, you are
  capricious;
Your lion and lamb
  can tease us.

BACKYARD OBSERVATION IN LATE MARCH

Robins listen to soil
  wakening under grass,
  hungrily peer and peck.

Male Blackbirds at bath
  sport with swell and swagger
  sleek and reddened shoulders.

Fair, felicitous Finches
  freshly perky and bright
  perch in pairs up high.

Grackles arrive by instinct,
  landing hungry and thirsty,
  eager to make their nests.

FELLOWSHIP AT THE FEEDER

Every season crowds gather,
feathered, finely-tuned to flocking;
answering the call to survive,
to fly, to flourish, to multiply.

Always the House Sparrows, immigrants
(some say illegal, despised by some,
feared by others— 'They're encroaching'
—watchfully peck among
shells to find the occasional seed.

House Finches—sweet singers, pretty red heads.
It is said they descend from escaped cage birds.
Surely they, of all the birds, know well
where the seeds come from, as they
perch on branches outside my kitchen window
craning necks toward me with expectant looks.

Chickadees and Juncos linger in winter,
Flycatchers sojourn in summer;
Barn swallows, determined to nest on front porch
swoop and catch bees in spring.
Flickers hide scarlet or gold
under their wings, but it shows
and shines forth brilliantly when they fly.

MAY 2020

On a bright blossomy breezy day
   my fears and sorrows blew away.
And in their place gentle hopes
   of fresh tomorrows came to stay.

SUCH A TREE

On a slope that rises
    from meadow to Rocky heights
    pine forested,
a short hike up the hillside
    and I stand among
    orange-barked trees.
One stands before me,
    defiant of extremes
    of seasons within seasons,
holding fast the slope,
    sheltering, sustaining
    insects, birds, squirrels;
beautifully scabbed, knotted,
    pocked, needled,
    rooting through rock,
turning soil's nutrients into
    seeded cones, scented sap,
    needed breath—
When I no longer breathe,
I'd be buried under such a tree.

HAIKU

ahh, green abundance
childhood's simple joys and smiles
sunshine happy dogs

sun: draw nectar flow
rain: replenish thirsty roots
flowers, bees: flourish

rabbits nibble leaves
in thickets stems seek shelter
flowers rise above

grace greases pathways
of creativity; who
is praying for me?

MOTTLES AND DAPPLES OF A FADING SEASON

In my backyard garden this October morning
Still-green grass is damp with last night's rain.
Along the flagstone path Lavender wafts.
In stands of fading glory Dill accosts and greets.
Smooth Squash hides beneath crisp, prickly leaves.

Bluejays call. Goldfinches peck at drooping Sunflowers.
Shrubs and rocks catch breeze-blown yellow leaves
Berries peek through cover, blushing as their moment comes.
Autumn composes in minor harmonies and moving tones
Songs of coming sleep, dreams of going homes.

DOWN BY THE SEASHORE

She savors seashells found on the seashore.
  And—
She shines beach stones found on the seashore.
  Will—
She sell what she finds down by the seashore?
  No—
She saves rocks and shells and hasn't room for any more.
  So—
Shouldn't she stay away from sheltered bays and seashores?
  Ha!

BEEN & BECOMING

A MORNING PRAYER

Expectant, I wake to meet you
    with the sunrise.
Trusting, I open my eyes to
    return your gaze.
Inhaling, I open my lungs to
    receive your breath.
Stretching, I welcome the new
    song you sing.

Listening, I wait on your words.
    Help me heed.
Calling, your voice speaks peace.
    Dwell in me.
Patient, you invite my response.
    Teach me, please.
Full wise, you light my path.
    Guide, I ask.

Present, you touch and fill
    my reaching hands.
Creative, you open ways
    to see, serve, speak.
May I live and work with you today.

TOGETHER

Let us live life
   moment by moment
Like the couplets
   of the Poet

Like harmonic
   songs we sing
Like the forth and
   back of swing

Here we improv
   like a jazz band
Here we twirl round
   hand in hand

Here your fifth chord
   calls me forth
Here my rhyme will
   echo yours

A PROCESS

Change may not come as hurricane blow,
    though it may.
A gusty breeze through opened window
    lifts papers aflutter.
A move from one house to another
    rearranges things.
A walk in the woods—spring or fall—
    breathes in new seasons.
A cleft in a circle of close-knit friends
    extends reaching hands.
A new awareness of being interlaced
    opens more windows.
Wind-blown papers settle, re-arrayed
    into fresh meanings.

WITNESS

You can tell someone 'It's true'
   till you're blue
   in the face.
But to show someone it works
   in you
   with your quirks
Gives them place, a space.

CAMPMEETING IN THE HILLS

By Eucalyptus-scented roads
   mid reverent stands of Redwood groves
   and trails downsliding to the creek,
   an altar lined to pray, to seek.

There the Invisible met the visible.
Soul and spirit grew soft, divisible.

Mingling prayers, smiles, tears;
   sweet Breeze eased crippling fears,
   supplanting questions, weights;
   planting seeds of lifelong faith.

GLORY

To a newborn king
   let angel voices ring.
'Glory,' saints would shout
   but now rocks cry out.
Glory sacrifices praise
   hides in a child's lay.*
None is worthy to express
   the glory of heaven's best.
But One revealed in Shekinah
   will have glory and honor.
So rise, shine, and give it!

*A lay: a song

THE SOUL LIKES SLOW

We are part of the
becomingness of
everlasting life!
    Life develops
    in cycles, seasons,
    a slow but sure process.

Love is patient,
Love endures,
Love hopes.

Sin grasps,
Sin interrupts,
Sin rebels
    against process,
    ignores promise,
    inhibits growth.

The soul likes slow.
Be free, my soul, from
clutter, hurry, distractions
    to
      go
    slow.

NO FORCED ENTRY

Surely God weeps with us
   feels and knows our limitations.
Do they limit God also?

Spirit-promptings, angel helpers,
   impressions flicker through
   our consciousness.
But we often can't hear
  or don't heed,
  enmeshed as we are
  in dying bodies.
Our wills uncoerced quaver
   unsure of God's
   lures, messengers, missives.

Many of our sufferings
   erstwhile-unheeded warnings
   might have prevented.
But God suffers alongside us
   still
   because of our pain,
   and also his own,
Not wanting to seize
   our inner ears,
   our deeper eyes.
Our core created hearts
   will never be forced with entry.
But Spirit will always be wooing.

SEARCHING

A spiritual search
Progresses in spurts

Stumbling round
The rocky ground

One can't measure
Steps to the treasure

Attention is honed
Attention then roams

A light flashes
A wave splashes

Will I find Thee?—
But ... You've found me!

WOUNDS

Wounded people
wound people.
Wounded, we all
(invariably, variously)
wound.
Jesus, finding himself
in woundable form
did not
wound
but plumbed the depths
of our woundedness
and let it
wound him
to the full extent
of harrowing
pain--
Sounding the depths
breaking the chains
for our gain
and his
Joy.

BE(E) DOING GOOD

As you buzz about (many things)
   are you singing, bringing out
   the fruitfulness of life?

As you wing from place to place
   do you cherish each colorful face
   in the garden of life?

As you pollinate far and wide
   are you ever calling forth
   the Creativity of Life?

As you gladly sip secreted nectar
   will you with honey feed
   both the world and the hive?

WAKING THE DEAD

Lord, have mercy...
  On those with wanderlust
  who seem to be lost;
  On those who, sleeping,
  surely seem to be dead;

Lure their trekking
  into seeking instead;
  Call forth
  the slumbering
  to wide-eyed trust.

Lord, in your mercy.

JESUS IN YOU?

Can your cozy Christ be cosmic too?
Does your personal Jesus love only the few?
Is your comfortable Jesus ever working to renew?
Is 'Jesus Loves Me' same as 'God so loved the world'?
Does your friend Jesus confront you with truth?
As deep calls to deep, what says Jesus in you
To Christ in others and in creation's milieu?

TIME & SPACE

W.A.I.

It takes some years, but rough bark heals
over sun scald. Trees grow tough where
trees are tough to grow. On those plains
freeze can come too soon or stay too late.

Sprouting there, you grew the strong-grained
character of a dirt farmer and railroad blacksmith
who stood the seasons, choosing patient
rootedness, arms lifted in trenchant, joyful service.

Your steadfast, sheltering care gave me soil,
shade to grow in, and even when transplanted
over and over, the leaves of fecund memories
have composted again and again into courage.

WINGS

If I had ...
a silvery box of fairy dust
    that I could trust,
I'd sprinkle sparkles light
    and sprightly
over every tripping rock
    littering your way
and turn them into bouncy
    springs to lift and
buoy you up on nimble wings.

I don't.
But I can stand and stir the dust
    with wings of prayer
and angels will hover there
    to guard your way.
Will you let their shining
    lighten your heart?
Will you trust the song they sing—
    in earth and sky—
let springs of silvery hope arise?

COURAGE IN

Encourage each one
  dear God
their heart desire
  to know;
distill the cry
  of 'help'
to nesting purr
  of 'with';
so they can face
  the day
and all it holds ...
  the night
and all it hides;
  to see
in darkness treasures,
  awake
with second sight.

BRIDGE

I missed seeing my mother grow old.
I won't see the young grow old.
Romantic poets didn't grow old.

But, old, I dream, see visions, opine,
connect with all in metaphoric time.

Poetry bridges now, future, past
and back, from young to old, and back.
The tides don't pause, their ebbs don't last.

Reckoning a dream that didn't and isn't?
Heed the beckoning, respond in the current.

MAKING

I made a friend.
We made a baby.
He made peace.
She made my day.

Our making is through
our bodies, our selves,
words spoken, thoughts shared,
remembered, together.

Not distant, detached,
but with, always with.

THAT CLOSE

How far is this life
   from the next?—
As far as these lines
   from the page behind,
With densely populated
   margins besides.

SHARED SPACE IN TIME

There's a heart space we still share
  as memories keep that time alive
    and dreams bring that place close.

I recall slight else of that class
  except our desks sat side by side
    and either, coming first, kept watch.

Time stood still in that shared space;
  with minds alert and senses intense
    our places merged into *our place*.

Meaning emerges with time spent
  as we measure time by places
    and space by time it takes.

Friendship fills both time and space,
  instantiates as *this*, *now*,
    gilds the past, rose-tints the future.

IT'S THE SOUL THAT'S SOLID

We hear that the soul in time leaves the body.
Come to its destiny, away it flies.
But perhaps it is the body that leaves the soul.
It dies.

The soul's earthly life expressed with a body—
which, though mortal, frail and fading,
has given it hands, feet, and mouth
to act, learn, speak—has ended.

One at the dying's bedside may hear
last words, last breath expressed with a sigh
and it seems the soul has wisped away
forsaking, giving the body to decay.

Mourners look down at the lifeless body—
not up to smile as the presence lingers,
of the ever-living loved one's soul
rising to be where it must now go.

Not to be too hard on us, though.
Life together's a precious gift,
rightly treasured, mourned and missed.
Through the body we've known that soul.

But there is more. The Soul is solid.
We wait in hope of life transfigured.
Earthly flesh gone, the person lives on
and will be re-membered, re-mattered.

GOD WAS THERE AND ...

Others' anger hid God's gaze.
Others' rejection felt like forsakenness.
Others' averted faces eclipsed God's countenance.
Others' disdain left you feeling unlovable.
Others' going away felt like aloneness.
Others' slaps blinded you to love.

But ...

God wasn't wrathful at you.
God didn't turn away from you.
God never frowned at you in disgust.
God never hid God's face from you.
God never struck blows at you.
God will never leave you.

FRAGMENTED

The taste
of the dust
of death
clung
to our tongues
for days

DEATH CAME CLOSE THAT NOVEMBER

Two November mornings
   brittle leaves lay cold
as Death and Life battled
   for young, for old.

Two heartbeats slowed
   as Finches huddled deeper
in evergreens that know,
   have witnessed the reaper.

A child's breath was labor—
   small seedling squeezed—
air chambers closing,
   hard bit the freeze.

A dry twig snapped—
   A man's spirit went—
Last breath expressed,
   an earthly life spent.

But boy gained breath!
   Drooping eyes awaked
as warmth chased the chill
   for Mercy's sake.

On gray November mornings
   young and old partake
in Death's cold moment
   before the Daybreak.

INSIDE & OUT

WORDS

Words let us down
and gems are muddied
as context distorts and obscures.

We let words down,
allow their sparkle to dim
from pretext, misuse and abuse.

Shine is shallow
in surface reflections,
but fire will glow from within.

New settings call
for refurbished gems
finely cut, polished and clear.

So mine deeper
for metaphors true
to reveal the hidden fire.

GATES

As I walk beneath silent pearlescence
    of evening sky
    in contemplative mood,
Pink clouds above the mountains split ajar,
    and ringing, singing gates
    open to golden glow....
But soon rumbling clouds threaten gloom.

By what dissonance do humans choose
    to bite into a poisoned lie?—
    or are we the bitten ones?
Lies erect walls whose gates deceive,
    stand vast and thick against
    revealing light, toneless,
Separate, defiantly hugging darkness.

Some bitten ones are smitten with
    what they believe waits
    behind shining gates—
Promises of escape and enhancements.
    Is that all we sinners
    can justly hope for?
Is Mercy—suffering, dying—prevailed upon?

Myths and misconceivings mingle,
    give birth to tales of
    torture, worms, fumes—
Convenient for consigning our scapegoats,
    hated enemies, sinners
    far beyond the pale.
Does weak, forsaken Love delight in this?

Is beautiful Love defaced,
    bared and impotent,
    kept by darker gates
Separate from all the beloved ones—
    distorted by power,
    reshaped by pride—
Shifting into wan and waning pleasures?

As luscious lips hide a rotten bite,
    dark gates' enticements
    lead to gnashing teeth.
As soft-lashed lids beckon with
    glances of invitation
    to adventure, they
Cloud dangerous orbs of burning lakes.

The biggest lie of lid or gate
    is that Hope
    has been waylaid
And endings can't be beginnings.
    A lie appears solid,
    a stone immovable.
But resounding horns crumbled Jericho's walls.

Pure sustained tones break crystal glass.
    Innocent melodies
    melt stony hearts.
A hellish barrier will not prevail!
    Not in false
    intimidating gates,
But in open, persuasive, singing Grace
    will I hope.

TILL WE SHOW OUR FACES

Evil has no face—
      It ghosts away what belongs to God
      (such as Fire, Light, Judgment).
Composited of lies, empowered by fear, feeding on hate,
dreadful and visageless like the Nazgul slain by Eowyn.
With a sword thrust to the mask's gap, "It" evaporates.

Faces are vulnerable—
      So we harden, veil, tat and smear them.
      (We have had faces masked for protection.)
Eyes, the windows of faces, can give them away.
A flicker of uncertainty, a blink, an escaping tear may
expose an Achilles' heel—or hole in the dragon's hide.

We hide our faces—
      to feel stronger, more invincible,
      powerful, mysterious, ambiguous.
In *Till We Have Faces* Orual veils her face, hides from Love.
Till we show our faces, Love longs for us to open
our true selves to One who pursues, woos and claims us.

Does God have a face?—
      Well, Moses saw its glow in the burning bush.
      Later, on the mountain, Moses' face shone. Then...
When the glow began to fade, Moses veiled his face.
Perhaps glory clothed Adam and Eve in the Garden....
Later, shadowed from God's face, they hid, sought cover.

Jesus gave God a face.—
    On the mount, Jesus' face shown with
    glory of transfiguring Light.
So God's face burns with pure fire to transfigure
what fear, trauma, and lies have deceived and imprisoned,
what resistance and rebellion have closed and obscured.

Do you fear your face?—
    Dread it appearing in a cloudy mirror
    through flimsy veil of self deceit?
Oh to be seen by Love's true and beautiful Face—
that which we are made to gaze upon, respond to—
like a healthy garden whose flower faces open to the sun.

To have a face—
    is to be real…
    knowable, reflecting, responsive.
Take off the mask, the veil has been torn.
Let yourself bask in holy Fireglow,
smiling, to finally know and be known.

UNHEALTHY ATMOSPHERE

May we never grow
  accustomed to this smoke,
  this red sun, this pink moon,
  this hazy shade of autumn.

May we crave fresh air,
  keep peering at gray horizons
  expecting mountain peaks,
  lake's far shore, lengths of fields.

May acrid particulates
  burning nostrils, biting eyes
  prompt us to heave
  our bucketful on the flames.

May memories live of
  galaxies singing masses,
  eagles riding sunbeams,
  sweet rain on clean grasses.

Would St Francis weep to see
  'Brother Sun, Sister Moon,'
  red faced, shrouded, peering
  down on forests burning?

May we seek obscured paths,
  find a way to fellowship,
  community. How can we,
  those blurred, be humanity?

QUESTIONS WORTH ASKING

Abortion (so personal, numbing ... but *gray*?)...
Senseless killing (is war ever necessary?)...
Death penalties (where's the capital in that?)...

Euthanasia (euphemism for 'mercy *killing*')...
Suicide (but the traumatized need mercy)...
Poisoning our food, air, water, soil, bodies...

Won't we do what we can to minimize these?
Justified and un-confronted, a culture of death
will affect who we are, alone and together.

'Who and what *do* we want to be?'
'Free.'
Free, you say?

But when my freedom impinges on yours?
Is all fair in love and war, really?—
When Love says 'vengeance is mine'?

Too complicated politically to fix?
Are Justice-and-Mercy scales broke?
Is Life not sacred? Is Death escape?

Will crumbling foundations give way in revolt?
Or, as we're deconstructing will we find
that we have broken ourselves against bedrock?

Then what and where and who will we be?

PLAYING GOD

They roll like a steamer, those
   who throw chunks of concrete along
   creek sides to shore up the erosion
   from their obnoxious wakes.

A never-ending stream they think
   they are, that will never dry up;
   but they don't realize their dryness
   of soul—or maybe they do—

So,
To feel more virile they rush rough
   over fresh, supine pools
   and virginal meadows, as if
   those lie there for them to seed.

CONFLICTED?

two jarring voices
compassionate, prophetic
stir and spar within

PERFECTING PERFECTIONISM

I know someone who wants to be
free of their perfectionism.
They think it's a generational curse
that can be cut off. Perhaps.

I wonder, though, whether
they are such a perfectionist that,
in their striving to be and act
and perform perfectly,
they see perfectionism as an
imperfection, and that is why
they want to be delivered from it.

SPIRALING

Circles should not break,
but my hand can't reach yours.

As a novel virus zooms 'round our world, playing its
sinister duck-duck-goose; making deadly sport of
kick-the-bucket or kick-the-can; holding us captive
on screens, divided in political cycles and false claims.

Daily spin and twisted messages assail at every turn.
Winds foment fire, smoke one day, ice the next.
As dust swirls, cries rise: *Lord of all, help us
see truly, breathe freely, touch warmly, hear clearly.*

May we again hold hands in a circle.

DOUBTING THE DARKNESS
(a dialog)

But it feels so real.
   Then where is the substance?
It shivers me with cold and fright.
   Push it back in the name of Light.

What light?! A myth. There's none here.
   The really real will soon appear.
No. This night thickens and sickens.
   Look! A rising glow up there—.

I can't. See, my shadow taunts and rents.
   A bent reed will not be broken.
Life has already torn me in pieces.
   Oh, I see a dormant, quickening force.

I'll lie below with face upturned.
   Your face reminds—I'll close my eyes.
Look again. Hope is rising.
   From whence the glow upon your face?

Simply a reflection of a reflection.
   This is a challenge I don't want.
I see a tiny spark in the smoldering.
   No. The wick has smoked and died.

My shadow darkens.
Do you not wonder why?
Await the Light and Life.
And so will I.

2020s VISION
(a prayer)

Help us...

to find our way forward,
    see spaces between words,
    perceive Presence amidst all things,
    focus on the wonder that wiser eyes seek.

to embrace ancient revelations of Truth;
    set sights toward the mountain top,
    envision potentials of the youth,
    take the next step in the fog.

TREASURES OF DARKNESS

Found there?:

Hope, wisdom, second sight,
    dreams, visions, focus
    sans bright distractions.

The true heart's dependency,
    the real self's desire
    distilled into one cry:

'Help' or 'Mercy' or 'Jesus,'
'Yes' or 'We' or 'With.'

Fruit then?

Perspective,
    patience, revelation, rest,
    consolation, awakening.

SINCERITY

Sincere people sincerely believe
　something is true
　that other
Sincere people sincerely believe
　is false.
　Ironically,
Sincerity may be honesty but
　not verity.

POETIC FREEDOM
or
UNBLOCKED

You say learned skills—
I say wounds healed—
  clear the way
  to say
  what's there to say.

THE DEEPS AWAKE

"I can't breathe."
Dirt needs oxygen,
soil must respire to
    live.
The concrete knee,
the asphalt grip
(foundations forgotten)
    leave
no passage for air
to roots, organisms...
From elemental deeps I
    heave,
send forth shoots
of ancient seeds
forced through cracks—
    a green gasp.

WHICH PRE-POSITION?

God is present to persons, things,
    each and all of creation.

Evil is not a presence as much as
    a rejection of Presence.
Evil comes *at* (with terror, lies,
    accusations, attacks).
God comes *to* (with peace, truth,
    affirmation, comfort).

In the midst of clamor, to which
    will we look and listen?

UNQUENCHABLE SHINING

The Lord is God and has given us light.
Darkness was upon the face of the deep.
Darkness threatened to swallow my soul.
But, 'Let there be light' was
spoken, the Word of creation;
and the sun shone and the day was.

In the world comes Light and
the Light is the Life calling forth newness,
illuminating the Way everlasting.
At evening time there shall be light.
'I am the light of the world'
shines in the darkness that comprehends not,
extinguishes not, can hide not.
So fear not.

CHURNED

Out of this milky, churning life
   where I find myself swimming,
   comes butter, sweet for giving—
   which, God help me, I will spread
   on your warm and broken bread,
And pair with your poured wine.

IN THE GRASSES

Mother would sneeze and leave
these native grasses wind waved.
But I lie in the earthy sweetness,
    nose itching—
    smiling, dreaming,
    imagining, remembering
an earlier pasture near fence, canal,
my sister's horse chomping, chewing,
then kicked, galloping across the field—
    hoofing the blades,
    shaking the ground,
    jumping the ditch.
A stallion cloud floats, lopes above,
and a bee buzzes now, checks out
my daisy chain of dandelions.

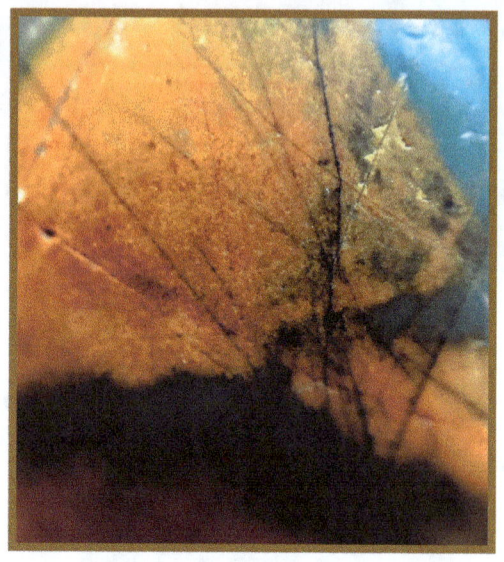

A closer look: macro photo of the design in a small beach rock.

NOTES

Shifting contexts and changing vistas marked the five years (2020-2025) during which most of these poems were written. Global pandemic, widespread wildfires and other natural disasters, political upheavals, deepening divisions, and lifestyles of isolation have intensified.

At the same time cycles of seasons have continued, as springs follow winters, days of dazzling beauty dawn, hope rises again and again.

Echoes of that time period may clash or clang, may ring or resound for each of us. But these years have certainly presented ongoing challenges and changes which have often felt tectonic. Many people--on both sides of every divide--seem tempted to despair.

While much of my poetry continues to express the experience of love, the assurance of faith, and the consolation of hope, these tougher times with precipitous paths and obscured views may elicit tougher poetry. Changing times call for renewed minds and transformed hearts and lives. Accordingly, uncertain times call for questions to be asked.

With that in mind, I offer comments on these poems (something I have chosen not to do in the past). A poem is not a lesson to pick apart, diagram, or analyze. It should be experienced, sat with, allowed to seep in. These notes are not necessarily explanations of the poems' meanings, but bits of the contexts in which they came to be.

I. SEEN & UNSEEN

13. AT THE POND

In a quiet moment I stood near a large pond in a city park of tree-shaded paths and Canada Geese. This, the most venerable park in our city had experienced many generations, seasons, and changes. People used to ice skate on this pond when winter temps were colder and freezes deeper. Some years a rookery of Black-crowned Night Herons populates the small, wooded island. Almost always people fish on the shores and children play nearby. Squirrels scamper and scold dogs on walks with their people. This time, as I watched reflections on the shadowed and rippled water, I felt acutely aware of the constant interplay of yesterday, today, and tomorrow.

14. DISPELLED

This did happen, I had this dream and these thoughts. "Perfect love casts out fear." And sometimes light comes to us, or we perceive it, by way of shadow.

Many literary references to the significance of shadows exist. I love these words in Tolkien's *The Return of the King*:

> "Sam saw a white star twinkle for a while. The beauty of it smote his heart, as he looked up out of the forsaken land, and hope returned to him. For like a shaft, clear and cold, the thought pierced him that in the end the Shadow was only a small and passing thing: there was light and high beauty for ever beyond its reach."

15. BEARINGS

St Bonaventure is often credited with the quote, "God is a circle whose center is everywhere and whose circumference is nowhere." Similarly, the psalmist declared, "Where can I go from your Spirit? Where can I flee from your presence? (Ps 139:7-12)."

16. THE LIGHT THAT IS

"I am that I am (Ex 3:14)." God isn't a being; God is being. Jesus said, "I am the light of the world (Jn 8:12)." Pure light begotten of pure being.

17. YOU IN ME AND I IN YOU

Deep calls to deep. We are made for God. We are restless till we find our rest in him. True freedom is found in beginning to attend to, turn toward, respond to God's continual wooing and calling and drawing.

18. BURNING BUSH TREE

This poem is based on a vision I had during prayer many years ago, which I recorded in a journal at the time. Years later, the title was inspired by a sermon that compared the two "trees" in scripture and what God accomplished through them in first making himself accessible and knowable, and then, in love, freeing us from sin and death.

20. WITHOUT MEMORY WE HAVE NO FUTURE
"We can't change the past, but we can change our relationship to it" I heard said. In inner-healing prayer ministry I experienced that. Others have changed their relationship to the past through psychotherapy. My father who was both a Christian minister and a licensed counselor, said this process involves being transformed through the renewing of our minds (Ro 12:2). A reconciled past gives us a foundation on which to build.

21. WE CANNOT STAY THERE
It's sad to see someone stuck in the past, controlled by the hurts and traumas that happened there.

23. RECOGNITION AND RESPONSE
This takes trusting the light. Or becoming desperate enough to be free of the darkness that one will turn and risk. Or maybe letting a friend take your hand and lead you there.

II. CYCLES & SEASONS

27. WONDERS OBSERVED
Startling, sparkling, silvery moments in my memory.

28. THE LONG COLD STARE OF JANUARY
Learning patience with Colorado winters, one day I stood looking out the kitchen window at the frozen landscape. I did feel like an indoor captive. But contemplating the beauty of the silent scene brought lines of this poem to me and transformed my perspective to that of enchanted captivation.

29. HOLY STILLNESS
I have written about the toads and salamanders that live in the deeps and come up in our basement window wells from late spring to early fall. It's strangely reassuring to see them, not unlike the spring plants poking up in the garden from last fall's seeds. When I am listening I hear a similar message as the liturgical words many Christian worshipers declare every Sunday: "Christ has died, Christ is risen, Christ will come again."

30. ENCHANTED FEBRUARY
    Parts of this poem are inspired by imagery in scripture and in poetry such as this: "I see his blood upon the rose / And in the stars the glory of his eyes / His body gleams amid eternal snows / His tears fall from the skies /...His crown of thorns is twined with every thorn / His cross is every tree" (by Irish poet Joseph Plunkett, 1887-1916).

31. AS DAYS LENGTHEN
    A chant of faith and hope.

32. HUMMING TOGETHER
    Humus, human, humble. Isn't the derivation and relatedness of these words interesting and revealing? In Hebrew, "Adam" (or "mankind") is directly related to "ground" or "dirt." One could say that to be a humble human is to be down to earth, in touch with reality, grounded. It is to remember that from dust we were created and to dust we will return. Creation and the incarnation of Christ have given breath, life, and dignity to our dust. Reason enough to be humble.

33. HYMN OF SPRING AFTER A LONG WINTER
    The cycles of seasons speak to us of hope and the truth, goodness, and beauty of things, if we listen.

34. THE INS AND OUTS OF MARCH
    My sister and I, both born in March (one year apart) always considered March "our month." We enjoyed chanting every March 1, "In like a lion; out like a lamb" (or the opposite, depending on fickle late-winter early-spring weather).

35. BACKYARD OBSERVATIONS IN LATE MARCH
    Seen out my kitchen window. ... And yours?

36. FELLOWSHIP AT THE FEEDER
    Another way of marking the seasons is observing the species and activities of birds that visit our yard and gardens.

37. MAY 2020
    This was two months after Covid-19 arrived in our city and I came down with it, suffering a long illness. A certain day in May I stepped out into the sunny front yard and stood under the Juneberry tree in full bloom, I can't explain the lift and

encouragement and lightness that came to me at that moment. Well, I have tried with this poem, haven't I? The white blossoms really did seem to communicate joy as they shimmied in the breeze.

38. SUCH A TREE
Rocky Mountain National Park is close enough to our home that we drive there regularly. I love the high-mountain wilderness park in all seasons. This was a late spring, early summer visit. We parked in a random spot and walked up a rocky rise dotted with conifers. I stopped before a strong, weathered, red-barked Ponderosa Pine. Encountering this tree, giving it my full attention, I was repaid with a fresh perspective and poem.

39. HAIKU
I don't often seek to employ traditional and classical poetry forms. I pay attention always to form, though, and try to work with it. It is said that structure actually increases creativity rather than stifling it.

40. MOTTLES AND DAPPLES OF A FADING SEASON
One fall I walked out into my garden and everything in the softer light cast by a lower in the sky sun (compared to summer), seemed to be teasing and winking and peeking.

41. DOWN BY THE SEASHORE
Playing with a tongue-twister verse from my childhood, this is a self admission and admonition that maybe there's a limit to how many rocks and shells I should collect. This hobby gives me joy though!

III. BEEN & BECOMING

45. A MORNING PRAYER
Words descriptive, not prescriptive.

46. TOGETHER BECOMING
Life is call and response.

47. A PROCESS
It seems one thing that is sure in life is change. This can be disruptive but also can be positive.

48. WITNESS

Showing is more effective communication than telling, certainly. And how can anyone argue with a personal experience or deny your story? Not that there isn't far more to life and faith than the mechanistic worldview of "what works." We don't measure results, but we can often observe them.

49. CAMPMEETING IN THE HILLS

I am blessed to have attended camps and campmeetings in the Santa Cruz Mountains most of my growing-up years in Northern California. More formative than I can fully appreciate, socially, spiritually and in growing my imagination.

50. GLORY

Some traditions emphasize the glory of God more than others. And with varying meaning and purpose. The second century theologian Irenaeus famously wrote, "The glory of God is a human being fully alive."

51. THE SOUL LIKES SLOW

God usually works slowly, as the anonymous author of *The Book of Privy Counsel* expressed: "Grace is rarely in a rush. It touches and changes us. But usually not as soon or as suddenly as we'd like."

52. NO FORCED ENTRY

Is there really ever freedom without constraints? For instance, this is true as the member of an era in history, a family of origin, a race, even a place. We may need to uproot from unhealthy or abusive situations. But, as persons finding ourselves unique, here, now, we cannot be free--or truly happy—if we fight against everything that has formed us, given us the gift of a life, provided us a container in which to grow.

53. SEARCHING

Does your life (I started to type "spiritual life" or "faith life" but really the spiritual is entwined with the physical life) feel this way sometimes? Keep on keeping on. I hold to Matt 6:7-8.

54. WOUNDS

Christ's wounds are efficacious.

55. BE(E) DOING GOOD

I have a complicated relationship with honeybees. Our relationship to things like service, good works, etc., can also be complicated. But at the same time it's simple: Just be good (with God's daily help) and do good (as you go about daily life). Stay alert, attend to the moment, listen before reaching (as I listen for the buzz of bees before reaching for a flower): these will increase goodness in and through you.

56. WAKING THE DEAD

In Luke 8:40-56, when Jesus healed Jairus's daughter who was thought to be dead, he told the people nearby, "She's not dead but sleeping." This encourages me to believe many who seem spiritually dead are actually "sleeping," They need to (and can and will) wake up when they hear Jesus' voice. And when they open their spiritual eyes and see him, they will want to rise and serve him as did the little girl. May it be so.

57. JESUS IN YOU?

Jesus Christ is not choosy or cozy. He is not tame. Like Aslan in *The Lion, the Witch and the Wardrobe*. When Lucy and Susan express fear about meeting Aslan, Mr. Beaver explains, "'Course he isn't safe. But he's good. He's the King, I tell you."

IV. TIME & SPACE

61. W.A.I.

For my maternal grandfather (through my mother's adoption), Walter A. Inskeep, from whom I received and felt unconditional love. An early and lasting influence in my life.

62. WINGS

A few years after I wrote the first stanza I added the second stanza and the needed words, "that I could trust."

63. COURAGE IN

One of the virtues we need the most in this life is courage. I pray for it for myself and for my loved ones. It can take courage to get up in the morning, to step into a church, a new friendship, a new start. Courage will take the next step. Courage is a gift. The Spirit of God is our great "en-courager." When we open our hearts, he pours "in courage."

64. BRIDGE
    Poetry is a bridge in many ways.

65. MAKING
    We are like God in this. God is three-in-one, always in community. In Genesis God said, "Let us make..." We don't create anything by ourselves, as one separate individual.

66. THAT CLOSE
    A faraway universe? Another dimension? Another domain?

67. SHARED SPACE IN TIME
    The relationship of, and experience of, time and space is endlessly interesting. So are memories that almost mysteriously stay with us and influence us.

68. IT'S THE SOUL THAT'S SOLID
    It is a mystery I certainly do not understand. But I do hope in the resurrection of the body. The title of this poem is an expression I heard from professor and philosopher Peter Kreeft in a recorded talk on his book, *Angels and Demons*.
    Another Christian writer and philosopher, D.C. Schindler has written, "The body is a manifestation of the person." And sacramental theologian Hans Boersma has said, "To remember is to make present." Historically, Christians believe and hope that, though our bodily members die, yet we shall be re-membered.

69. GOD WAS THERE AND ...
    I am convinced that God is always actively with us, suffering alongside us and working for our good. I have prayed with people who were so mistreated as children that they can hardly come to a place of trusting God and believing he loves them. I have also seen light shine into dark memories, bringing freedom and release and hope. God's presence and goodness are hidden to us by the sins of others as well as our own.

70. FRAGMENTED
    These lines first appeared in my novel, *Face to Face* (Cladach, 2004, now out of print. A new edition will be released in 2026).

71. DEATH CAME CLOSE THAT NOVEMBER

Inspired by the emotions of actual experience. During November one year my brother in law, Curt, died. It was traumatic for my sister to find him in the morning, lifeless. A week or two earlier I was caring for two grandchildren alone when they and I (unexpectedly and as an emergency) had to spend a night in the hospital as I held the younger one upright in my lap all night so he could breathe, be comforted, and be treated for pneumonia. This experience is hard to think about let alone write about. Both events were unexpected, not the kind of surprise you want. But the poem came to me (perhaps to help me deal with the memory). And I hope it will speak to someone else who has faced a similar sense of horror and helplessness.

V. INSIDE & OUT

75. WORDS
The challenge before writers, especially poets.

76. GATES
Against Love that never fails / How can a ghostly gate prevail?
I find it helpful to consider that it is God's unrelenting love that is the aggressor against the gates of hell (not vice versa). And they cannot hold, they cannot stand against that Love (perhaps they will break themselves against it). On the cross Jesus won victory over sin, death, and the grave. Christian tradition says in the time between his death and resurrection, he visited the "underworld" and harrowed hell. So look away from hellish things—to Jesus!

78. TILL WE SHOW OUR FACES
Why do people stare at evil and hide from love? Fear.

80. UNHEALTHY ATMOSPHERE
During summer/fall 2020 wildfires raged in the West from the Pacific coast to Colorado, and some days our mid-day sky darkened with orangish smoke. Ash fell on everything. Now, five years later at this writing, a different sooty smokiness is darkening the atmosphere of our human society. Moral clarity is obscured. Flames of fear and hate increase as charity decreases.

81. QUESTIONS WORTH ASKING

We parse, capitulate, and make excuses. But surely life is sacred. Also keep in mind that God's forgiveness and mercy will always flow to us when we turn, reach out to, open to him.

82. PLAYING GOD

Where are the respectful, the humble? Jesus said, "Blessed are the meek, for they shall inherit the earth (Matt 5:5)."

83. CONFLICTED?

Jesus followers "shouldn't" have inner conflict, right? But call it what you will, life in a world where the presence and image of God is distorted, presents us with situations that elicit conflicting impulses in response. *Even if we agree that love must always be our motivation*, do we mean forebearing, reaching love expressed in compassionate acts, or tough, speaking-the-truth love? Surely both have their place and can't really be separated.

84. PERFECTING PERFECTIONISM

Here's an example of how difficult it can be to parse out our motivations. Hebrews 4:12 says the Word of God is a two edged sword, effective in separating bone from marrow, soul from spirit, discerning the innermost thoughts and intentions of the heart—humanly impossible processes.

85. SPIRALING

Written, obviously, during the Covid-19 pandemic. Honestly, I don't think all hands have again joined in their circles, or not the same circles as before. In the past I have been in prayer circles where we held hands. As children we often held hands in circles for games and ceremonies. In recent years I have been encouraged, though, attending churches where people hold hands while saying the Lord's Prayer together and shake hands during the passing of the peace.

86. DOUBTING THE DARKNESS

For those who find themselves in dark places of their own choosing or as the result of trauma: I like to prayerfully envision rays of true, healing Light shining into their milieu, psyche, dreams, etc., in such a way that the darkness will no longer feel like a protective, safe hiding place.

88. 2020s VISION
    Will we commit to, work with God in this?

89. TREASURES OF DARKNESS
    Whether that darkness is nighttime or sleeping or dark periods of life (see Is 45:3).

90. SINCERITY
    I think of the metamodern word, "Ironesty" (both sincerity and irony), which describes something neither simply sappy nor completely cynical.

91. POETIC FREEDOM OR UNBLOCKED
    Personal experience. Can you relate?

92. THE DEEPS AWAKE
    1) If you were alive and awake during 2020 you will recognize allusions here. 2) Since childhood I have had a fascination with little plants growing up through cracks in cement or asphalt. Soil needs oxygen because plant roots require it for respiration. Recently I have learned a little about the wondrously complex communities of microorganisms (bacteria, archaea, fungi) living in earth's soil.

93. WHICH PRE-POSITION?
    As a poet and writer, I am fascinated with those often taken for granted parts of speech, prepositions. So little and seemingly insignificant, yet making such a difference.

94. UNQUENCHABLE SHINING
    Truly good news!
    Since youth my favorite biblical writer is the apostle John. The church tradition in which I was raised made much of his writings. He wrote of Christ as Light, Life, and Love.
    One line of this poem is prompted by a memory of my mother's funeral when the preacher spoke from Zech 14:7: "At evening time there shall be light." The preacher drove through many miles of snow that sad winter day to be with us and offer words of comfort and hope. In his message he described his experience as a young man

returning home after time far away, in the darkening, cold night. He told how his heart rose when he spied a light in the distance shining from the window of his mother's farm house kitchen window.

I consider my mother to be among the cloud of witnesses who I believe continue to pray for us. In a sense her light guides me home. How great then is the Light of Christ. Dark times, thick night, bewilderment and grief cannot extinguish it. That Light leads us to Life because of Love. Let it lead you home.

95. CHURNED

Thoughts, experiences, visions, dreams, relationships, insights, conceptions, perceptions. All churn in this liquid life. One floats by and I may snatch it, but it slips away. Several adhere and begin to congeal into expressible words, then melt into vagueness again. I smell, taste, see that richness is there, blended into the milky flow.

I am utterly, udderly needy. "But I have calmed and quieted my soul, like a weaned child with its mother" (Ps 131:2). In God's presence, I become stilled, I let the cream rise. The wise richness separates from the thin whiteness, to be skimmed. Then shaken to a soft solidity that glistens, even when cut, spread, melted, it will flavor and give adherence and coherence to clear expression.

96. IN THE GRASSES

During the pandemic I attended a poetry reading and workshop online through the English department of my alma mater, Point Loma Nazarene University. We attendees were given a poetry prompt of a short video showing native grasses waving in a light wind. Having grown up among the golden summer grasses of California, the video images invoked personal, piquant memories that knit themselves together into this picture/poem.

ACKNOWLEDGMENTS

I thank God for:

- My husband, Larry, who read a proof of this book and told me frankly, "This may be your best work yet!" Through the years we have ministered in music and missions together; planted gardens together; reared children together; played with grandchildren together; plus I watch him play basketball and he reads my poetry and blog posts.
- All our family, including my sister Beverly, for their interest and affirmation.
- My fellow authors and poets at Cladach Publishing who make up a talented, supportive community..
- My Facebook, Wordpress, and Substack friends and followers for the feedback and encouragement when I share my poetry with them.
- Author and ministry leader Christine Sine who first published several of these poems at Godspace Light: "Be(e) Doing Good," "I Can't Breathe," "The Long Cold Stare of January," and "Holy Stillness."
- The living Christ, in whom all things hold together; and through whom and for whom are all things (Col 1).

ABOUT

Catherine Lawton is a prize-winning poet who also writes fiction, creative nonfiction, and memoir. Her work has been published in various print and online publications through the years. This is her third book of poetry.

Cathy has served authors and readers as editor-in-chief at Cladach Publishing for 25 years. She and her husband, Larry, reside in Colorado (they previously lived in Northern California). Larry and Cathy value time spent with their children and grandchildren. They also find joy in friends, gardening, travel, seashores and mountains.

ALSO ENJOY THESE POETRY COLLECTIONS BY CATHERINE LAWTON

GLIMPSING GLORY
POEMS OF LIVING & DYING, PRAYING & PLAYING, BELONGING & LONGING

66 poems.
Original color illustrations.

"Terrific second book of poetry with beautiful illustrations. Some poems are of nature, some spiritual, some mourning losses, and some celebrating joys. I will keep it on my bookshelf to return to again and again. Bravo!"

–Mary Langer Thompson

REMEMBERING SOFTLY
A LIFE IN POEMS

65 poems.
Original color illustrations.

"The hopes and prayers of a life given to love come through strongly. Fresh scenes also draw us back to the visual. The light and lively artwork gives yet another lovely touch to this book."

–Mary Harwell Sayler

Order from your favorite bookseller or at CLADACH.com.

www.ingramcontent.com/pod-product-compliance
Lightning Source LLC
LaVergne TN
LVHW021120080426
835510LV00012B/1765